Risks and THRILLS!

Contents

Real World

Flood Alert!

by Christine Taylor-Butler

Why Do Floods Happen?

Floods usually happen when there is too much rain. The ground cannot absorb the water, and riverbanks overflow. In coastal areas, strong winds and high tides can cause floods.

In cities, heavy rain can cause drains to overflow. The water spills into streets and houses. Sometimes floods last a few hours. Sometimes it can take weeks for the water to go away.

REAL LIFE

5th–6th December 2015
Storm Desmond hit the UK, causing devastating floods. The rainfall in this storm broke all UK records, and Honister in Cumbria received 34.1 cm in just 24 hours.

Around 5,200 homes were flooded, and more than 43,000 people were left without electricity. Rescue workers helped evacuate thousands of people from their homes.

The cost of repairing the damage caused by the floods is estimated to be £500 million.

Surviving a Flood

Floods can destroy roads and bridges. Strong currents carry away houses and cars. Floodwaters can make tap water undrinkable and dangerous.

Power and phone services may be cut off for weeks. People are often trapped in their homes. Boats and helicopters are used to rescue them. Rescue workers search for lost pets too.

How to Survive

When flood warnings are issued:

- Move to higher ground.
- Gather tinned food and drinking water.
- Don't cross deep water on foot or by car.
- Turn off electrical items.
- Use a battery-powered radio to listen for warnings and information.
- Fill sinks and baths with clean water.

Fixing the Damage

Cleaning up after a flood is a big job. Pumps are used to carry water away from the town. Once the water has gone, people have to clean their houses. Furniture and other belongings are often ruined.

Did You Know?

- Water covers about 70 per cent of Earth's surface.
- In 2013, floods killed more people than any other type of disaster.

JOB PROFILE

Electricians help restore power after a flood. It can be a dangerous job. Electricians must find safe ways to replace the power lines without getting hurt.

From A Railway Carriage

by Robert Louis Stevenson

Faster than fairies, faster than witches,
Bridges and houses, hedges and ditches;
And charging along like troops in a battle,
All through the meadows the horses and cattle:
All of the sights of the hill and the plain
Fly as thick as driving rain;
And ever again, in the wink of an eye,
Painted stations whistle by.

Here is a child who clambers and scrambles,
All by himself and gathering brambles;
Here is a tramp who stands and gazes;
And there is the green for stringing the daisies!
Here is a cart run away in the road
Lumping along with man and load;
And here is a mill and there is a river:
Each a glimpse and gone for ever!

The Red Lady

by Benjamin Hulme-Cross

Part 1

“It was a cold, dark, stormy night and the wind was wailing,” began Grandpa.

Kal and I looked at each other and grinned. We’d been on holiday for only a few hours and already Grandpa was telling ghost stories.

“A gale was blowing and there was no moon – just the sort of night the wreckers had been hoping for. *The Black Rose* would be struggling in the wind, the captain not quite sure of his position and eager to find shelter from the storm.

“The wreckers stood in a line along the clifftop – the very same one you can climb up to along the path that runs past the front gate of this house. At the agreed time, they opened their storm lanterns, signalling ‘safe haven’ to the passing ship. Sure enough, the captain of *The Black Rose* was fooled. He guided his doomed vessel towards the lights until she hit Hell’s Teeth, the line of rocky spikes that you’ll see tomorrow, just beyond the headland.”

"What happened to the crew?" Kal asked, round-eyed. He was always more affected by ghost stories than I was.

"The crew perished, the cargo washed up on the beach and the wreckers made off with it," Grandpa continued, "and that would have been the end of the story, were it not for a very peculiar intervention.

"There was one survivor, you see. A man named John Hawkins was rescued by a mysterious woman and he then went and alerted the coastguard. The wreckers were found out and they met their deaths at the gallows. John Hawkins spent the rest of his life trying to find the woman who swam out to the rocks and pulled him to safety. All he could say about her was that she wore a red cloak, and that she disappeared as soon as he was safely ashore. He never found her – but, from time to time, there is a report of a strange lady in a red cloak roaming the rocks near here. They say she is still looking for survivors from that fateful night."

The next morning, we went down to the small beach. There wasn't much else nearby. It was a rugged, tough place with huge cliffs, dark caves and gargantuan boulders strewn around everywhere. It was fresh and clear and cold, and we had the place entirely to ourselves.

"Just us and the Red Lady – eh, Amy?" said Grandpa, tickling my ribs.

I grabbed a bit of driftwood for a walking stick and walked along the tidemark, making ghostly wailing noises. Grandpa just smiled.

Later that afternoon, we told Grandpa we were going to go and explore along the clifftops.

"See if you can spot the Red Lady," he said, chuckling.

We ran out of the house and climbed steeply up a rocky, scrubby slope, following the rising coastline to the top of the cliff on one side of the beach.

From up there you could see for miles and miles – and we forgot all about the ghost story. The sky seemed five times bigger than normal, with huge clouds scudding over, driven by a strong wind. The sun was setting already and, above the horizon, the sky was ablaze with every shade of red and pink you could imagine, and more besides.

Five minutes further along, we came to a great slab of rock that sloped steeply down to a tiny, sandy cove. We scrambled down on hands and feet like crabs. Soon we were skimming stones into the waves and howling like wolves.

I stared out at the horizon just as a cloud moved and the setting sun hit my eyes with full force. Dazzled, I turned away so that I was facing the back of the cove. For the briefest moment, I thought I caught a flash of red. *My eyes must be playing tricks on me after looking at the sun*, I thought.

Part 2

On the afternoon of the third day, Grandpa fell asleep on the sofa and we decided to go back to the little cove. We left a note telling Grandpa where we had gone, and then ran out and retraced our steps. The wind was strong, and the waves were really hammering against the shore, sending up huge fountains of spray as they slammed into the rocks on either side of the little cove.

The clouds were heavy. There was no sunset to dazzle and delight us that evening, just a gradual darkening and a growing chill. We'd been playing for less than an hour when we decided it was time to go back to the house. The tide was coming in, and the cove was being slowly swallowed up by the sea. I led the way to the slab of rock that sloped up to the cliff top – and that was when I realised we were in trouble. Dry, the slab had been easy to clamber up. Soaked in sea-spray, it had become treacherously slippery.

I made a few attempts to find purchase for my feet on the rock but, as soon as I tried to put any weight on them, they slid away and my knees cracked into the slab. I looked up and saw that the rock was wet to a height of at least five metres. There was no way we were going to climb it until it had dried out.

Then it started raining.

"We'll have to find another way up," Kal said. We both looked around but we could tell straight away that the slab was the only safe route. Tears began to sting my eyes and I could see Kal was beginning to panic too. We shouted ourselves hoarse calling for help, but the roaring waves rolled closer and closer.

Once again, my eye was caught by a flash of red. I stared hard, and grabbed Kal's arm.

"Look!" I breathed.

At the back of the cove was a huge boulder and, through the now driving rain, I thought I could make out the shape of a woman in a red cloak on top of it, hood pulled up. She beckoned and her mouth seemed to be speaking, though I could hear nothing over the noise of the wind and the waves. Kal recoiled in horror, and I must admit I was shaking a bit. Then the woman disappeared, down behind the boulder.

"Whoever she is, we'd better follow her," I said.

Kal shook his head, his eyes wide with terror.

"Listen," I said. "Even if she is a ghost, which she isn't, she rescues people, remember?"

It took a few minutes, but in the end Kal saw that we had no choice. We climbed up to the top of the boulder and saw that there was just enough space to drop down behind it. In front of us, faint footprints led into a narrow, dark cave.

I took a deep breath and began walking forward, every muscle in my body tensed. I could barely see a thing, and was feeling my way along the rock on each side with my finger-tips. Kal was breathing in short, rough gasps behind me. And then I tripped and fell, and Kal tripped over me, and we each let out a shout.

We got back to our feet, both of us nervous wrecks now. I took a few more steps and saw that the cave had a second opening. We scrambled towards it and, from there, we were able to clamber up the rocks back towards the path. As we reached the top, Kal made a frightened noise and grabbed my hand.

In front of us was a lady in a red coat, its hood pulled up against the rain.

"Goodness me!" she said, sternly. "What have you been doing down there in this weather?"

I could have cried with relief, and Kal breathed out a huge sigh. There was nothing ghostly about her after all.

"Thank you so much!" I said. "We'd have drowned if it wasn't for you showing us that cave."

She gave me a puzzled look, and what she said next I've never been able to explain.

"What on earth do you mean? I've never seen you before in my life!"

Haiku Year

by Rachel Rooney

small green spears appear
gardeners reach for their forks
a battle begins

it's wet play again
I watch raindrops playing tag
behind steamed-up glass

we paint our toenails
roses wear their best petals
butterflies visit

somewhere in the fog
the road slowly disappears
both of us are lost

only the robin
perched on the recycling box
thinks it's still Christmas

snow falls overnight
the world is newborn and soft
cries break the silence

The Cake Catastrophe

by Anna Humphrey

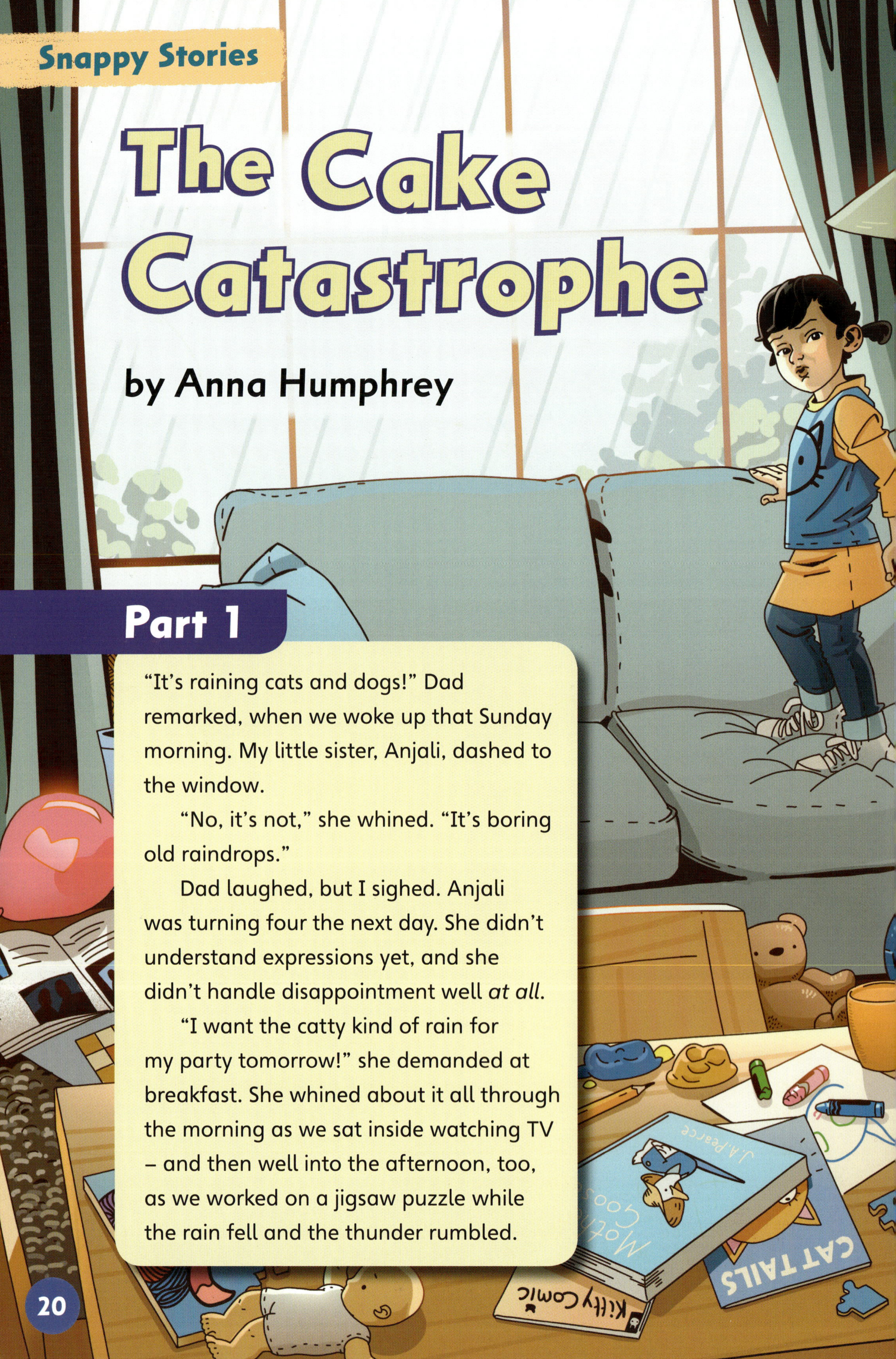

Part 1

"It's raining cats and dogs!" Dad remarked, when we woke up that Sunday morning. My little sister, Anjali, dashed to the window.

"No, it's not," she whined. "It's boring old raindrops."

Dad laughed, but I sighed. Anjali was turning four the next day. She didn't understand expressions yet, and she didn't handle disappointment well *at all*.

"I want the catty kind of rain for my party tomorrow!" she demanded at breakfast. She whined about it all through the morning as we sat inside watching TV – and then well into the afternoon, too, as we worked on a jigsaw puzzle while the rain fell and the thunder rumbled.

By the second day of the big storm, Anjali was driving me crazy. I wasn't even glad when Dad said school was closed because of the rising water. In fact, I was more than a little worried. Sure, it meant no maths test, but it also meant another day stuck inside with Anjali. Plus I could tell from the way Dad kept frowning as he checked the news reports on his phone that this was way more than your average downpour. According to him, parts of the county were without power and, in some areas, people were being told to evacuate their homes. Luckily, our area was still relatively safe.

Because Dad was staying at home, my friends Sam and Evie got dropped off at ours while their parents went to work. They had to wade through ankle-deep water to get to the front door, but I was glad to see them. I wasn't so glad when my dad put us straight to work.

"There might not be a party for Anjali at all, if this rain doesn't let up soon," he said to us softly, so my sister wouldn't overhear, "but we should get ready just in case. Why don't you three make some decorations?" He made it sound like a suggestion, but it was really more of a command. "I'll be in the kitchen, baking the cake."

"The catty cake!" Anjali squealed, running past. My sister wanted everything to be 'catty' themed for her party – from cat-shaped balloons to sparkly cat-ear headbands for the guests.

Long after Dad had finished icing the cake and had put it in the cellar fridge, Sam, Evie and I were still working on the cat headbands.

"Look!" Evie shouted, all of a sudden. She pointed out the window. There, cruising down the street, was our neighbour Mr. Connolly … but he wasn't in his car. He was rowing a boat!

"Boaty!" Anjali cried gleefully, as a bolt of lightning lit up the sky.

"Oh no," Dad said. He turned on the radio for the latest news report. It wasn't good. The flood waters had breached the nearby river's banks. Everyone on the south side of the river was ordered to evacuate their homes and head for a shelter on higher ground. That included us!

First, Dad called Evie's and Sam's parents and said we'd meet them at the shelter – and then (despite Anjali's tears) he called all the party guests to cancel. Finally, he got busy moving our electronics and some old photo albums to the attic. Meanwhile, he told me to pack overnight bags. "Only the essentials," he instructed. Sam and Evie came to help.

"Okay, Anjali!" I called, as my friends and I headed back down the stairs a few minutes later. "I've got your teddy and PJs. Time to go."

I waited, but there was no answer – because there was no Anjali!

Part 2

Sam, Evie and I searched all my sister's usual hiding places, but there was no sign of her. It wasn't until my eyes landed on the cat-themed party decorations on the dining-room table that it hit me.

"Anjali's cake!" I said, running towards the cellar. "She must have gone down to get it."

"Anjali!" I cried, when we got half way down the stairs. There, standing on a chair in front of the fridge, was my little sister. She was holding the plate with her cat cake on it, and all around her was murky brown water. It reached almost to the top of the chair legs.

"Stay there! I'm coming to get you," I said – but Sam held me back.

"Wait. It might be dangerous." He motioned to the socket where the fridge was plugged in. Sam was right: electricity and water didn't mix.

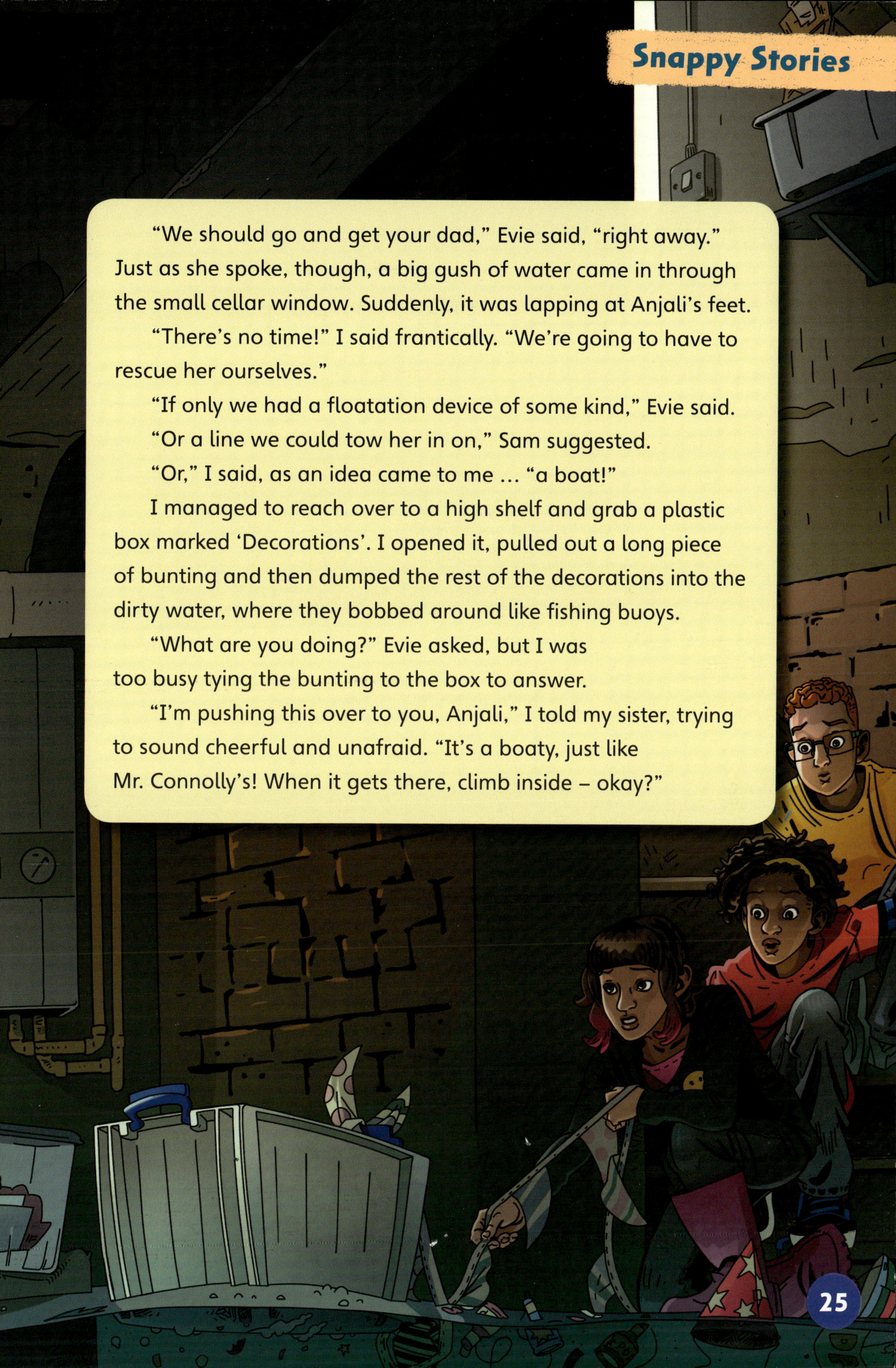

"We should go and get your dad," Evie said, "right away." Just as she spoke, though, a big gush of water came in through the small cellar window. Suddenly, it was lapping at Anjali's feet.

"There's no time!" I said frantically. "We're going to have to rescue her ourselves."

"If only we had a floatation device of some kind," Evie said.

"Or a line we could tow her in on," Sam suggested.

"Or," I said, as an idea came to me … "a boat!"

I managed to reach over to a high shelf and grab a plastic box marked 'Decorations'. I opened it, pulled out a long piece of bunting and then dumped the rest of the decorations into the dirty water, where they bobbed around like fishing buoys.

"What are you doing?" Evie asked, but I was too busy tying the bunting to the box to answer.

"I'm pushing this over to you, Anjali," I told my sister, trying to sound cheerful and unafraid. "It's a boaty, just like Mr. Connolly's! When it gets there, climb inside – okay?"

My sister nodded, but then (as far as she was concerned) the *real* disaster struck.

"My cake!" she wailed, as the cat-shaped confection slipped from her hands and landed in the water with a plop.

"Anjali! It's okay. We'll get you another cake," I lied. "Just get in the boat." Finally, she climbed into the plastic box. Working together, Sam, Evie and I reeled her in – and not a moment too soon. Just as she reached the stairs, the chair on which Anjali had been standing was engulfed by water.

With our hearts racing, we ran up the stairs to safety.

◇◇◇

Half an hour later, though (after we and Dad had waded through knee-deep water in the driving rain to reach the flood shelter in the village hall), Anjali was still crying about that cake.

"You know ... " Sam paused, and looked around the big, drab room where we were gathered. He wrapped his arms around himself and shivered. "This *is* a pretty rotten way to spend your fourth birthday."

He was right: the mood in the shelter was grim, to say the least. Families were huddled together on camp beds, kids were crying and everyone was soaked to the bone.

"Wait – I have an idea," I said.

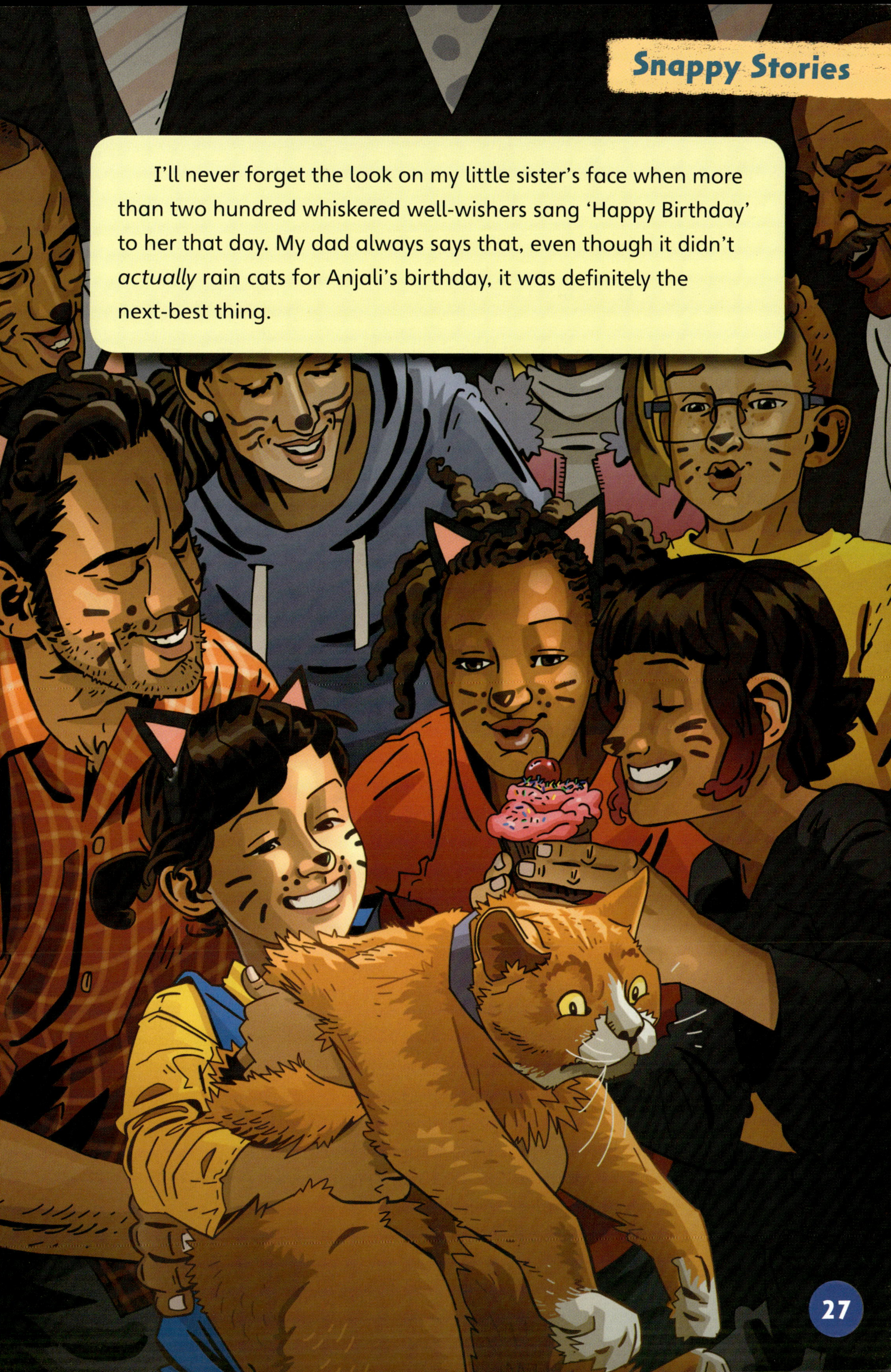

I'll never forget the look on my little sister's face when more than two hundred whiskered well-wishers sang 'Happy Birthday' to her that day. My dad always says that, even though it didn't *actually* rain cats for Anjali's birthday, it was definitely the next-best thing.

Switched!

by Tanya Lloyd Kyi

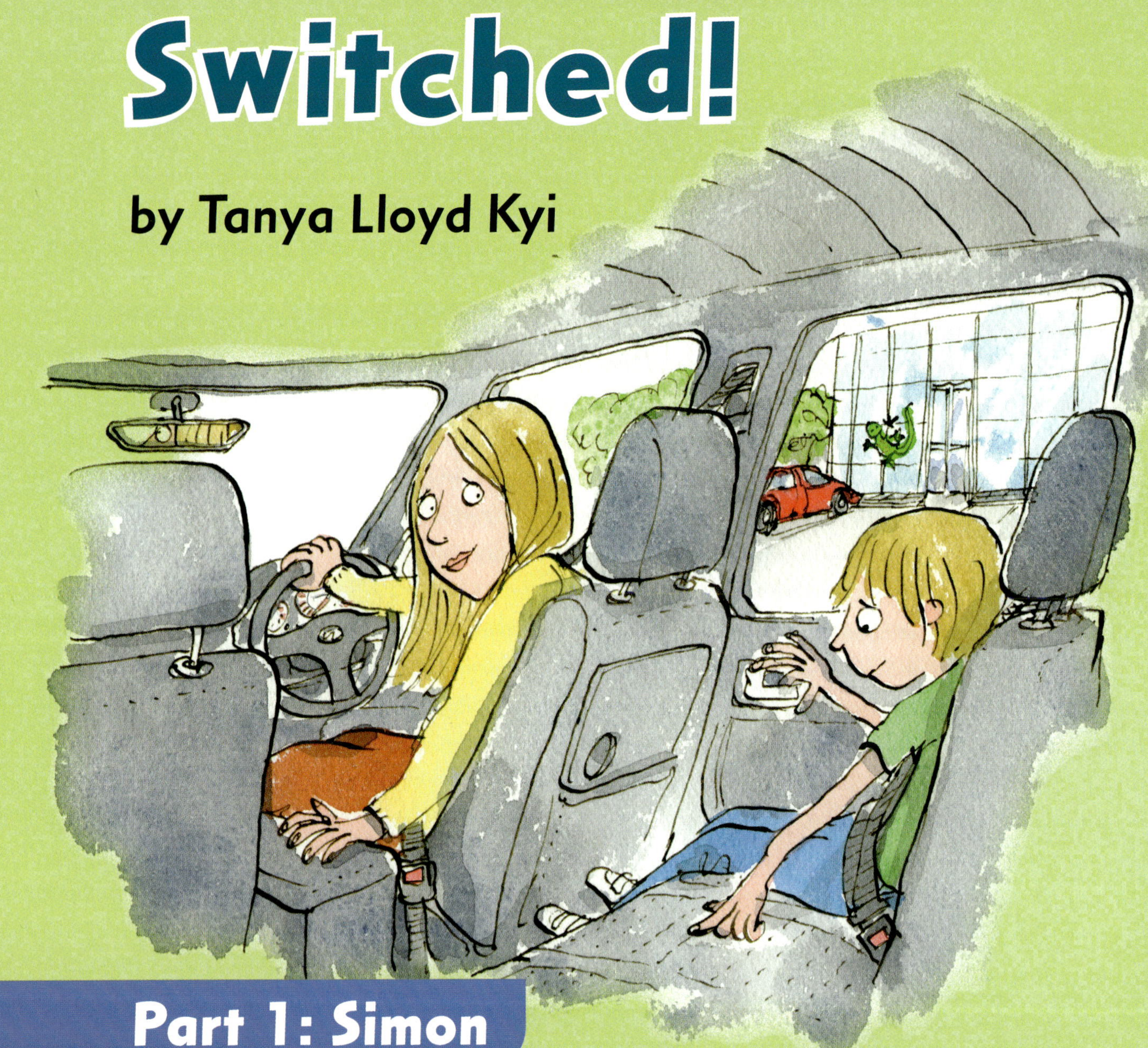

Part 1: Simon

When Mum drops us off at the climbing gym, Rob bounds from the passenger seat like a Labrador retriever set free in a park.

"Hurry up, Science Boy," he calls over his shoulder.

Still slouching in the back seat, I consider claiming a sudden stomach ache. Or tendonitis. Or leprosy. This is climbing lesson three, and the first two were horrible.

"Do you want me to come inside with you?" Mum asks.

I shake my head. I'm not going in there with my mum, like a little kid.

These lessons were her idea of a bonding experience. She doesn't understand why two twelve-year-old boys wouldn't be instant best friends. But Rob and I have basically ignored each other since we met a year ago, and things didn't improve when he and his dad moved in last week.

"You'll be like brothers, now," Rob's dad boomed.

That was ten minutes before Rob moved his stuff into *my* bedroom, covered the walls with football posters and broke my microscope with his basketball.

"It's fine," I say, and look away again. "It's not really my sort of thing. Rob is … we're just different."

Mum leans between the front seats. "I doubt you're as different as you think, Simon." She gives me a small smile. "This has been a change for everyone. If you just give each other time – try to imagine what it's like in each other's shoes."

Sighing, I haul myself out of the car. Mum gives a little *toot-toot* of her horn as she pulls away.

As I pull open the gym doors, I spot Rob already hanging by his fingertips from a handhold on the warehouse wall. A rope runs from his harness, through a clip near the ceiling, and down to the harness of his instructor, Finn. Finn is 'on belay': planted in a wide-legged stance on the floor, ready to catch Rob if he falls.

"Simon!" My own instructor, Meg, greets me with a smile. She's about my mum's age, but her biceps are bigger. They're bigger than Rob's, too, actually.

Her grin seems so sincere that I find myself pulling on my harness without complaint. I stuff my feet into my climbing shoes.

"They still squish my toes." Okay – maybe one complaint slips out.

"They're supposed to feel that way," Meg says, leading the way onto the mats. The whole warehouse is a fake cavern, thick with chalk dust. Up each knobby wall, coloured handholds mark various climbing routes.

Rob is now high above the mats. I groan. My new 'brother' is some sort of orangutan.

"I'm not sure climbing's going to work out for me," I say, following Meg reluctantly. "I'm more of an intellectual."

She hands me my harness, taking in my expression as I look up at Rob. "You know, I bet you could be at least as good as Rob, with time," she says.

Behind her, I see Rob slip from his perch. The rope arcs behind him for a moment – and then pulls taut, jerking him like a rag doll.

At that exact instant, *my* body jolts. My head whips back, the rope yanks at my waist, and the air swooshes from my lungs.

I open my eyes to find myself dangling above the gym floor. Below me – way too far below me – I see … me.

How did I get up here? Especially if I'm still down there? This is not scientifically possible.

"I'm not letting you quit," Finn hollers. "I told you last week: no more excuses. Reach out and grab that hold."

It takes me a minute to realise he's talking to me. It takes a minute more to figure out what he wants me to do. But the choice between dangling in mid-air or swinging myself to the wall seems like a simple one. Soon, I plant my toes on two miniature ledges and wrap my hands around a chunky green hold.

Panting, I loosen the fingers of one hand and flip it over. It's covered in callouses. My forearms bulge, the muscles and tendons visible under the skin. This confirms it. Possible or not, I'm stuck in Rob's body.

I glance down.

"Rob?" I barely whisper it, but he seems to hear me. He takes the rope from Meg and expertly twists it through his harness. "Hold on, bruv. I'm coming up," he says.

I watch my own body climb toward me.

Part 2: Rob

That feeling – as my fingers peel from the handholds and I know I'm going to fall – leaves me shaken. It takes me a minute to realise I'm safely on the ground, staring up at my own form on the wall above. *Wait … what?!*

I'm shaken again, but I'm a practical guy. I don't waste a lot of time wondering how I got into Simon's skinny body, all elbows and knees and barely a muscle to be seen.

"Hold on, bruv. I'm coming up," I say. Even my voice is different. It comes out higher than I expect.

I grip the wall. *Don't look down. Breathe. Focus on the next hold – the next move.* These are the things I whisper to myself every time I climb. Now that I have arms the size of liquorice bootlaces, I'm twice as sweaty.

"What's going on?" Simon-in-my-body hisses when I reach him. You'd think he'd be happier. He just got a major upgrade.

"Let's go," Finn calls. "The longer you wait, the harder it's going to be."

He's not the most sympathetic teacher in the world.

"I think we should go home," Simon says.

"Finn's not going to let you down," I tell him. "I've been stuck at this part of the wall for the past two weeks. If you want to go home, you'll have to get up there first." I'm still breathing heavily, but I manage to point to the striped green hold that marks the very top of the route. Then I force in another breath.

"Stuck? I thought you were the big climbing machine," he whispers.

My newly stringy biceps shake.

"The only way down is up!" Finn calls.

"Just get it over with," I tell Simon – but he has a strange look in his eyes.

"You're scared of heights," he says.

"Don't be stupid." I glance down. *Big mistake.*

"Why do you do this to yourself? Why would you climb, if you're scared of heights?"

I glare at him. "I thought this would fix it, okay? I thought I'd get used to it. And, if I can't climb, I can't apply for outdoors school next summer."

Simon's actually grinning now, which is like watching myself grin in the mirror, except wackier. Also, I have a pimple on my chin I never noticed this morning.

Focus. I grit my teeth. "Look, if you get my body to that last hold for me, you can have the whole desk in our room. And the bookshelf, too. I'll keep my stuff off them."

"Oh, I'll need a little more than that," he says.

"For one climb?"

He considers. "If I get to the top, you tell Mum we're finished with climbing – and we want to take coding lessons instead."

"Coding? Are you serious?"

"Computer club is at ground level."

He has a point. "Deal."

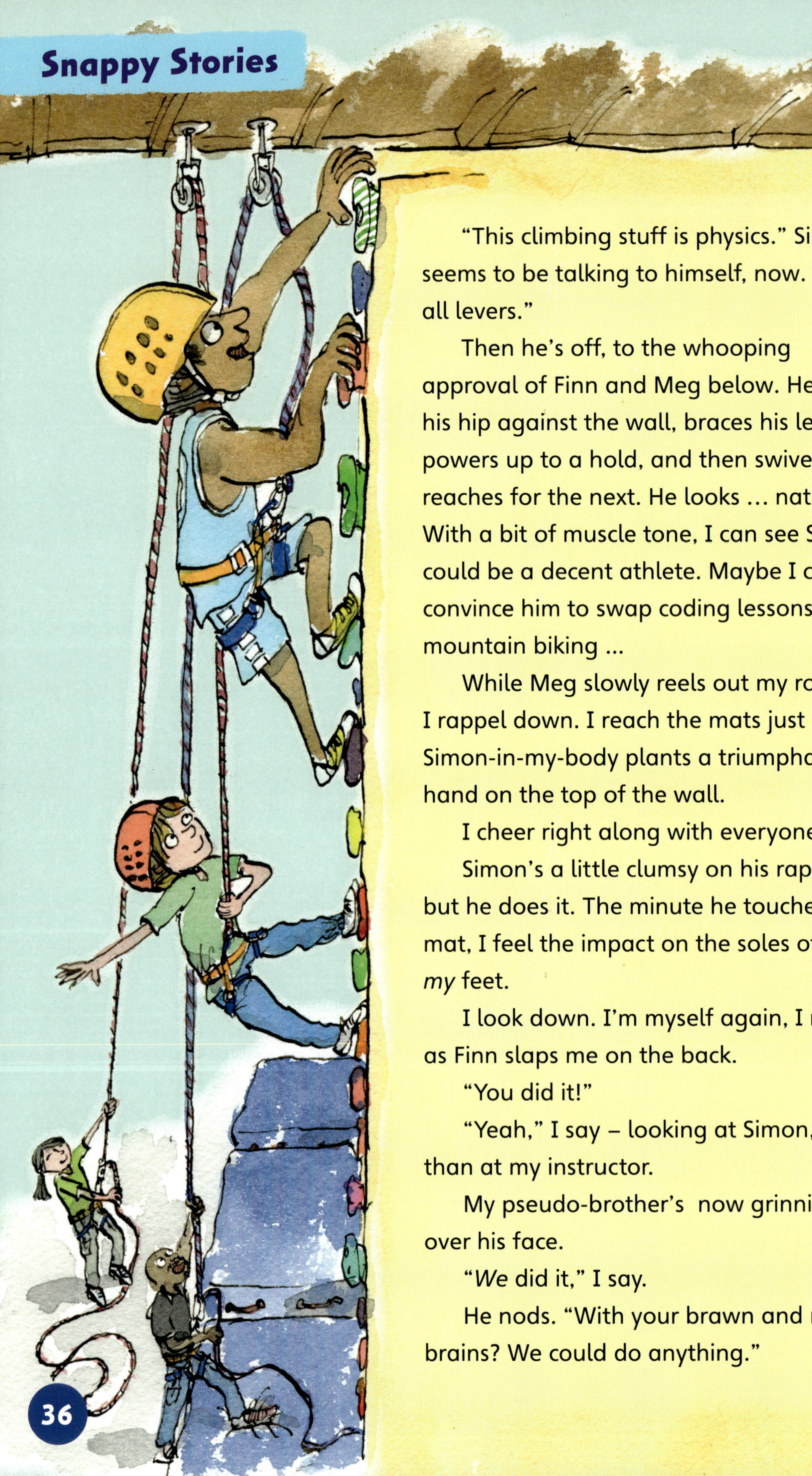

"This climbing stuff is physics." Simon seems to be talking to himself, now. "It's all levers."

Then he's off, to the whooping approval of Finn and Meg below. He tucks his hip against the wall, braces his legs and powers up to a hold, and then swivels and reaches for the next. He looks … natural. With a bit of muscle tone, I can see Simon could be a decent athlete. Maybe I can convince him to swap coding lessons for mountain biking …

While Meg slowly reels out my rope, I rappel down. I reach the mats just as Simon-in-my-body plants a triumphant hand on the top of the wall.

I cheer right along with everyone else.

Simon's a little clumsy on his rappel, but he does it. The minute he touches the mat, I feel the impact on the soles of *my* feet.

I look down. I'm myself again, I realise, as Finn slaps me on the back.

"You did it!"

"Yeah," I say – looking at Simon, rather than at my instructor.

My pseudo-brother's now grinning all over his face.

"*We* did it," I say.

He nods. "With your brawn and my brains? We could do anything."

Once we've stripped off our gear, we push our way out of the gym doors together and stand blinking in the sun.

"So, coding?" I ask, raising an eyebrow. "Is that, like, computer games?"

"It can be," Simon says thoughtfully. "There are still rules and strategy."

"Like sport, then?" I smile.

Simon pauses. "Yeah … not so different, I suppose," he answers – and we both grin.

Pukka! by Paul Mason

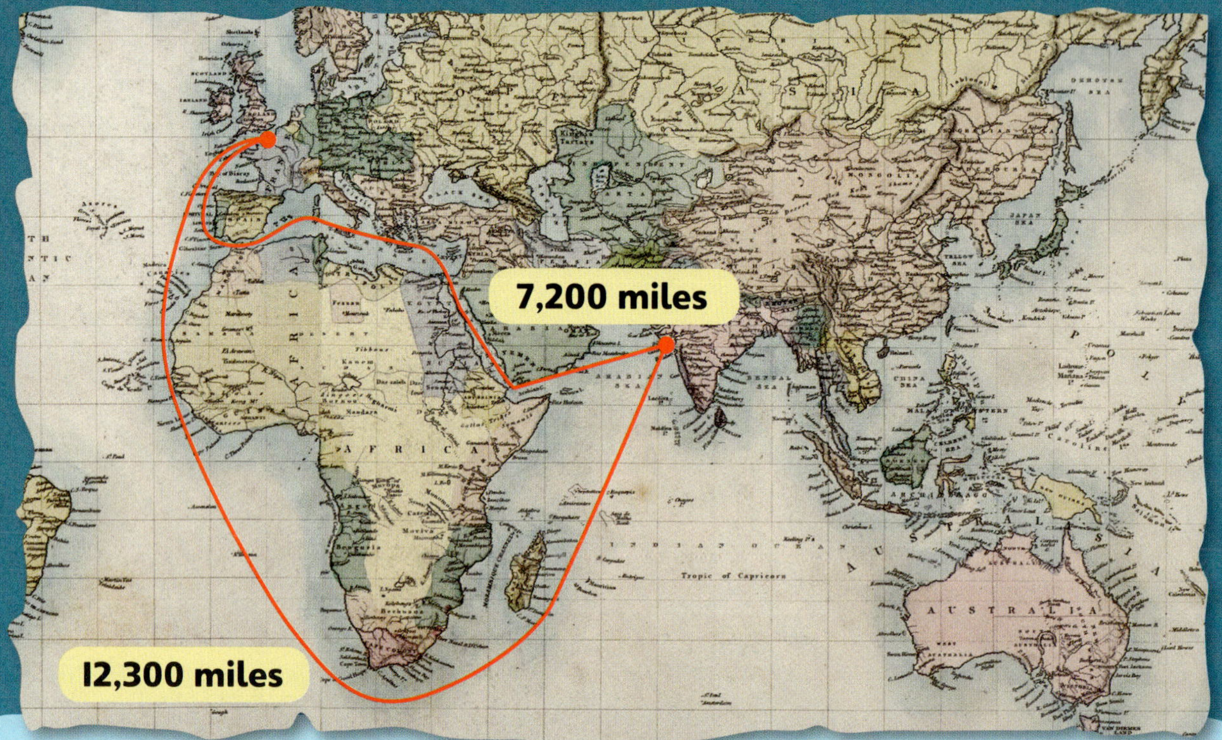

In the 1600s, the first trade ships of the East India Company sailed across the world and reached the shores of the Indian subcontinent. The people who travelled between Britain and India for trade, leisure or to live started centuries of shared history between the two countries.

In India, British people came across a world they had never encountered before: a continent of new names and words. It's not really surprising, then, that the English language is full of words with Indian origins. Let's have a *dekko* at some – or a look at some, as we'd say without the Hindi word *dekho*!

There are six words of Indian origin in this passage. Can you spot them all? (To see the answers, turn to page 40.)

We paddled upriver in our dinghy, through thick jungle.

Home was a subject often on the minds of British people who were overseas. They dreamed of heading back to 'dear old *blighty*', that very British word for *home*. Actually, it's from an Urdu word used to describe the travellers to their land: *bilayati*, meaning *foreign* or *English*.

But which words might you be more likely to use today? Well, perhaps you had a *curry* last night, made with mango *chutney*. We can thank the Tamil and Hindi languages for these words: *curry* comes from *kari* in Tamil, and *chutney* from *catni* in Hindi, meaning *sauce*.

Before bed, you might have taken off your *dungarees*, got into the shower to *shampoo* your hair, and then put on your *pyjamas*. In Hindi, *dungri* is a kind of rough cloth, and *champo* means *press* or *massage*, while *pay jamah* means *leg clothing* in Urdu.

There are so many English words of Indian origin that a famous dictionary of them was published in 1886 – and it was 1,000 pages long! That really is a *pukka* fact – which is a word with both Urdu and Hindu roots, literally meaning *ready* but usually used to mean *genuine* or just *very good*!

At last, we reached a bungalow not far from the bank.

Published by Pearson Education Limited, 80 Strand, London, WC2R 0RL.

www.pearsonschools.co.uk

Designed by Sarah Fountain
Illustrated by Sarah J. Coleman, Bonnie Pang, Tracey Knight, Carl Pearce, Rupert Van Wyk and Clare Elsom

First published 2017

21 20 19 18 17
10 9 8 7 6 5 4 3 2 1

British Library Cataloguing in Publication Data
A catalogue record for this book is available from the British Library

ISBN 978 0 435 18617 3

Printed in the UK by Ashford Colour Press

Acknowledgements
The publisher would like to thank the following individuals and organisations for their kind permission to reproduce their photographs:

(Key: b-bottom; c-center; l-left; r-right; t-top)

123RF.com: Sarah Allison 39; **AlamyImages:** Andrew Findlay 3tr, Andrew Johns Photography 6-7, keith morris 6bl, Kraig Lieb 2-3; **Getty Images:** ANDREW YATES / AFP 4, Christopher Furlong 5br; **Shutterstock.com:** auremar 7br, RTimages 38

Cover images: *Front:* **Alamy Images:** Andrew Findlay

All other images © Pearson Education

Answers for page 39

These are the words of Indian origin found in the passage:

Bungalow: from the Hindi word *bangla*, meaning *belonging to Bengal* (it was used to describe a type of cottage built for early European settlers there)

Dinghy: from the Hindi word *dingi*, meaning a rowing boat

Jungle: from a Hindi word that was first borrowed from Sanskrit, *jangala*, meaning *rough and unfarmed*

Loot: from the Hindi word *lut*, meaning *rob*

Thug: from the Hindi word *thag*, meaning *swindler* or *thief*

Veranda: from the Hindi word *varanda*, which means *railing*